UNDERSTANDING KARMA

Your Pathway to Healing, Forgiveness, and Freedom

Martina E. Faulkner MSW

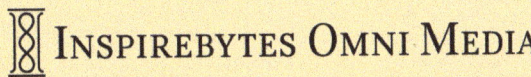
INSPIREBYTES OMNI MEDIA

Understanding Karma: *Your Pathway to Healing, Forgiveness, and Freedom*

Copyright © 2025 Martina E. Faulkner

This publication is published and distributed worldwide in the English language in the following formats:

ISBN Paperback: 978-1-953445-72-8
ISBN E-Book: 978-1-953445-73-5

This book was printed in a manner that minimizes its impact on the planet and the environment. Learn more at: www.inspirebytes.com/why-we-publish-differently/

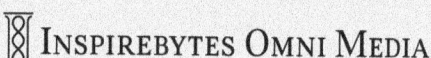 INSPIREBYTES OMNI MEDIA

Inspirebytes Omni Media LLC
PO Box 988
Wilmette, IL 60091

For more information, please visit www.inspirebytes.com
Graphics and photos: Canva Design Pro

> "How people treat you is their Karma; how you react is yours."
>
> — Wayne Dyer, PhD —

Introduction

Karma is a word many people use without truly understanding the depth of its significance. It is often invoked when someone has felt wronged or wishes to place blame on others. It is also used to invoke penalty with detachment.

Most notably, though, Karma is often referred to in a singular, externalized direction, as in: "Karma's only a bitch if you are." (Most people don't consider themselves to be a bitch, but may easily identify others as such.)

As one of the Universal Laws, however, Karma is devoid of these human-based judgments and subjectivity. Karma simply is. In these pages, you will learn the What, When, Who, Why, Where, and How as it relates to Karma. More importantly, you will also discover tools you can use to help you heal your Karma, leading to healing, forgiveness, and freedom—the ultimate goal.

If you've ever been curious about how Karma really works, or if you have wanted to have a better understanding of Karma and how you can apply this understanding in your own life, then you're in the right place and this is for you.

Welcome!

Contents

PART I: Understanding Karma

On our journey through life, or through lifetimes, we accumulate Karma—both good and less-good. This is part of being human. "Earth School" (as it is sometimes referred to) is about learning. We (our souls) are here to engage with life in a way that supports our evolution and growth, so that the collective can also grow, and so that we can return to oneness.

Life, however, can get messy in all the (very) human ways. Sometimes we behave kindly and sometimes we don't. Sometimes we receive things that hurt, and sometimes we receive things that heal. Throughout our life, we are both the recipient and the perpetrator.

By understanding Karma and how we can engage with it on a regular basis, we get to have an impact on how often the good outweighs the less-good. We get to choose how we show up for ourselves and others—which is the best gift we can both give and receive.

What is Karma?

"Don't judge each day by the harvest you reap but by the seeds that you plant."
— Robert Louis Stevenson —

What is a Universal Law?

Karma is one of the Universal Laws, as we understand them. In my opinion, it is most similar to the Law of Energy, which states simply that "everything is energy." Karma, like energy, is both tangible and intangible. We can know it and experience it, we can impact it, but we can't always understand or quantify it. It just is—which is part of what makes it a Universal Law.

Types of Karma

Though it seems to be universally understood and applied across multiple religions, practices, and beliefs, Karma can be looked at through different lenses, including both the physicality of life and lifetimes, as well as the more intangible aspect of thought. These variables serve to provide parameters and understanding in Karma's application, but they don't change the underlying rule, which ultimately is about action.

"Realize that everything connects to everything else."
— Leonardo da Vinci —

Karma and
The Golden Rule

"Do unto others as you would have them do unto you."

The Golden Rule

Some variation of The Golden Rule can be found in virtually every belief system on the planet practiced by humans. For many, it provides a moral compass that has its basis in an ethical understanding that we are all connected and part of something greater, whether that's society, the species, or the planet as a whole. The rule is set forth as a guiding principle of behavior that invites the individual to consider the consequences of their actions before they are undertaken.

Karma as a Boomerang

The best analogy to understand Karma and how it works is the boomerang! In short, the concept is simple: Whatever you put out will ultimately come back to you... eventually. For Karma, the most important words in that statement are: "ultimately" and "eventually."

When Does Karma Happen?

"Like gravity, karma is so basic we often don't even notice it."
— Sakyong Mipham —

This Lifetime vs. All Lifetimes

In Hinduism, there are different words for Karma based on lifetimes. Specifically for "this lifetime" the word is: Prarabdha. This refers to the Karma that is sown and reaped during this specific time of being alive. The word that refers to Karma that is carried forward from a past life is: Samchita. And finally, the word for Karma that awaits the soul in a future lifetime is: Kriyamana.

Conversely, Buddhism considers Karma to be part of the cycle of birth and rebirth, with no specific delineation between lifetimes. Therefore, the soul is free from all Karma when it no longer needs to reincarnate.

These variations are the most traditionally understood ideas when it comes to Karma. Commonly (and more often than not), they are blended into one principle that is best expressed by the old adage: You reap what you sow. Presumably, this is true regardless of which lifetime you are in. It's from that more general perspective that we will focus on understanding Karma.

"I believe in karma, and I believe if you put out positive vibes to everybody, that's all you're going to get back."
— Kesha —

Alignment and a Divine Blueprint

Navigating Timelines

For many, the concept of multiple lifetimes where Karma is concerned can be seen as both overwhelming and (potentially) a cop-out. If our actions have no known consequences in this lifetime because they can be carried over, what's the point of managing our Karma account now? The short answer is: Because it's the best option... for everyone.

If the Universal Law of Karma is to be understood and accepted, then another old adage is also relevant: There's no time like the present!

Without being privy to the Divine Blueprint of the Universe and its ultimate wisdom in timing, the best option is to do our best now, and always. That way, we know we are helping ourselves to be free of karmic patterns in the future, as well as helping make the world a better place for everyone along the way.

Altruistic? Yes. But no less powerful or important.

"Every action of our lives touches on some chord that will vibrate in eternity."
— Edwin Hubbell Chapin —

Who Can You Have Karma With?

"The ones you judge today may be the judgments you endure tomorrow."
— Unknown —

Karmic Relationships

The short answer to who you can have Karma with is: Anyone, but not necessarily everyone in your life. In truth, it's a bit more probable that you have Karma with people who are consistently in your life so that you can work on the Karma together. These can include:

- <u>Soul Family</u>—Most often these are people who are your actual family and friends.
- <u>Soul Pod</u>—Typically, these are "adjacent" people in your life, like coworkers.
- <u>Soul Mirrors</u>—These are people whose Divine Plan aligns or intersects with yours.

For the most part, you can look at karmic contracts and all of these relationship groups through the lens of: Reason/Season/Lifetime. Each of the above groups will fall into one of these categories.

Furthermore, people within these groups can move between categories once the Karma is completed. For example, a lifetime person can become seasonal, just as a reason person can become lifetime, etc.

Lifetime Karmic Relationships

Lifetime Karmic Relationships are the most common, which means that these are the relationships we have with people who are consistently in our life. It also means that the karmic healing and lessons can come and go in waves. Like a spiral, we move through these patterns with this person, continually leveling up in between periods of neutrality, calm, and peace. These relationships allow us the most grace as we heal from Karma, as these are the people who stay with us, regardless of what's happening.

Reason-Based Karmic Relationships

These relationships are the ones that serve a single purpose to help us learn or remember something we needed to overcome. You know it was a Reason-Based Karmic Relationship when the person is simply no longer part of your life once the lesson was learned and the Karma was allowed to resolve. Unfortunately, many people fall into the trap of trying to make the person stay (which creates new Karma), rather than seeing it for the gift it is.

Seasonal Karmic Relationships

Seasonal Karmic Relationships serve to create opportunities for growth during a specific period of your life. Once the period is done, the relationship usually ends or the person can move into one of the other categories.

*"When you plant a seed of love,
it is you that blossoms."*
— Ma Jaya Sati Bhagavati —

Where Can You Work On Your Karma?

"My actions are my only true belongings.
I cannot escape the consequences of my actions.
My actions are the ground upon which I stand."
— Thich Nhat Hanh —

Karmic Healing Is Always Available

Karma can be worked on anywhere at anytime. It is not limited to a specific place, time, or environment. In fact, healing Karma is most effective when it becomes part of everyday life.

When you view Karma as a way of being, rather than a task to be achieved or crossed off a list, you will experience greater freedom and peace more easily, and more readily. Healing Karma is about aligning your behaviors through shifting your mindset.

Though some have likened having a karmic mindset to being selfish—doing good in order to receive good—nothing could be further from the truth. However, if that is what first brings you to the table, that is still a place to start. Starting is what matters.

Once you have started to shift your perspective on Karma, you will begin to feel more balance as you experience a greater connection to your own being and to the world around you. This will lead to feelings of empowerment and peace, ultimately resulting in the freedom and joy so many seek.

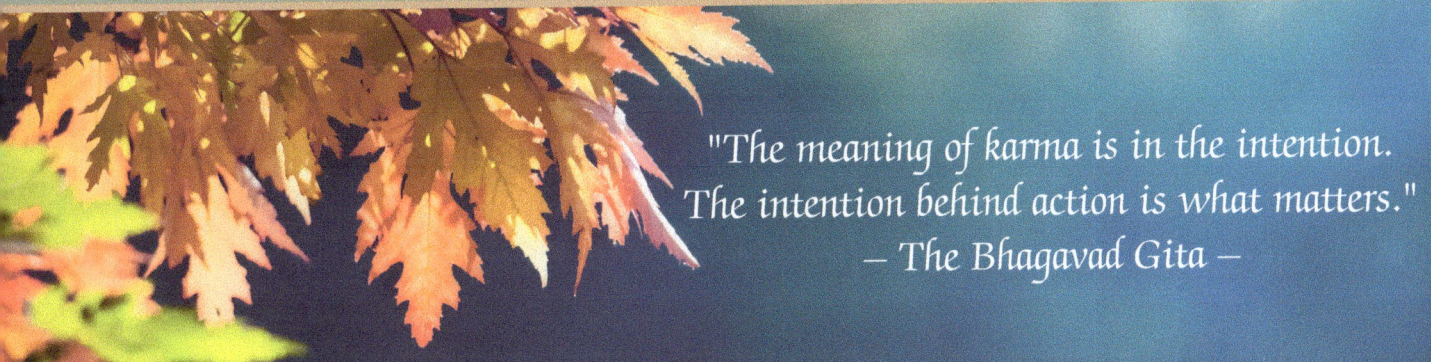

Best Practices

As with everything, there are Best Practices for understanding and healing your Karma. These can include both solo and group activities, such as meditation, volunteering, journaling, and more!

Solo Activities

Individual endeavors to heal Karma often involve activities that are both introspective and reflective. This can include: therapy/counseling, journaling, meditation, and movement, such as yoga.

What all of these activities have in common is the opportunity they create for deeper connection to self. Knowing yourself better is what allows you to show up in life better. Thus, providing more opportunity to heal your Karma. It really can be that simple.

Group Activities

Participating in groups can be a beneficial method of healing Karma, because they provide a safe space to explore our connections, feelings, and thoughts. They also allow for feedback and support, unlike solo activities.

Some group activities can be deliberately focused on creating healing, such as retreats, support groups, or counseling. Whereas other activities, like volunteering, can create an environment for connection, which can also lead to healing.

Why Do We Have Karma?

"When you see a good person, think of becoming like her/him. When you see someone not so good, reflect on your own weak points."
— Confucius —

What Is the Purpose of Karma?

Karma is a tool that helps us evolve as a species, on an emotional and spiritual level. While physical evolution is highly tangible and visible, karmic evolution is somewhat more subjective, unless you look at it with a much wider perspective.

For example, since the industrial revolution, many countries have adopted laws that prevent the exploitation of children as workers. This could be viewed as a karmic evolution for the species. But where did it begin? Most likely, it began with individuals. All it takes is one person to question the way things are—to see things in a way that could be better—for different decisions to be made.

Karma is about action, not just thought, as it's the different actions that create different results, thereby impacting one's Karma, or the Karma of an entire society.

 *"Your believing or not believing in karma has no effect on its existence, nor on its consequences to you. Just as a refusal to believe in the ocean would not prevent you from drowning."*
— F. Paul Wilson —

Understanding that our actions are not isolated events and can create ripple effects throughout our communities and world is a first step in understanding how important it can be to be mindful of one's own Karma.

Individual Karma

Individually, our souls are on their own journey toward oneness. What does this mean? It means that we have come to "Earth School" to learn, remember, and apply those lessons in ways that show our spiritual evolution. Whether you understand that it's for one lifetime, or many lifetimes, the goal is the same.

In order to achieve this goal, we need opportunities to show what we have remembered, as well as opportunities to learn new things. In most cases, these opportunities come as life lessons, such as: patience, tolerance, kindness, and love. The greatest tool we can use to learn these lessons, therefore resides in the ability to take perspective. By seeing ourselves in another's shoes, we have the ability to understand and make better decisions —for ourselves and for the whole.

Ultimately, this elevates everyone and everything as we create a better world, together.

"Our lives are not our own. We are bound to others, past and present, and by each crime and every kindness, we birth our future."
— David Mitchell —

How Do You Heal Karma?

"What you hate, you re-create; and what you bless, you put to rest."
— Eric Micha'el Leventhal —

Requirements for Karmic Change

Though many people may believe that they need to go to a shaman or other esoteric practitioner to help them heal their Karma, this is not true. Healing Karma is predominantly an inside job, meaning it has to start from within. Practitioners can provide guidance, but that is all. As such, healing Karma requires four specific things:

Willingness
Guidance
Deliberate Attention
Consistency

Willingness

When a person is ready—truly ready—to begin working on their Karma, willingness is the first step. A commitment to show up, take perspective, and create change is the only way to begin. It also requires some measure of humility to take this step as one must also admit that they have most likely treated others as they have been treated, somewhere along the way.

In fact, one of the greatest hurdles in healing Karma is the belief that it is a one-way street. Many people find it hard to accept that they may have wronged others as they feel wronged, but it's the first step in understanding how Karma actually works. The rebalancing is always in progress.

Guidance

As previously mentioned, one can find assistance in healing Karma from external sources, such as esoteric practitioners. This help can come in the form of teaching tools, sharing learned wisdom, and providing support. It is good to remember that a practitioner cannot do the work for you.

Deliberate Attention

In order to heal your Karma, you must first raise your awareness to your existing habits and behaviors so that you can pay deliberate attention to changing them.

Consistency

Once you have identified what it is that you need to change, the key to healing is to remain consistent. To heal Karma, one must shift their presence. This is a process (it's not a one-and-done endeavor). Being consistent in your commitment will lead to healing.

"The best way to find yourself is to lose yourself in the service of others."
— Mahatma Gandhi —

What if I Already Wished Harm?

"You cannot do a kindness too soon, for you never know how soon it will be too late."
— Ralph Waldo Emerson —

Undoing Harm

It is possible to undo or interrupt the creation of Karma if you have recently wished harm on another. The keywords here are: "recently" and "interrupt." They are intertwined due to their nature. They are also somewhat subjective.

"Recent" can mean anytime from the last few seconds to within one day. The more recent the behavior, the greater the success in reversing it. "Interrupting" means stopping in transit. In this case, stopping in creation. There is a reason why Karma isn't immediate: It allows for humans to be fallible... and to change their mind.

Steps to Interrupt, Reverse, and Undo Harm

While there may be more ways to address this situation, here are two of the simplest ways to interrupt any harm you may have directly or inadvertently wished upon someone:

"Cancel and Purify"

Sometimes our emotions get the better of us and we say things we regret or don't really mean. Sometimes we mean them but think better of it later. To help interrupt this event, as soon as you are able, say: CANCEL AND PURIFY.

This is something I learned a long time ago from a trusted friend; it's a way of telling the universe that you didn't mean what you just thought or said, and asks for help in neutralizing the thought or statement.

Lifting Others Up

If it has been longer than a few minutes or a day, you can take a different approach and make amends. Amends can look like actually atoning and asking for forgiveness, or it can look like changing your actions and engaging in life-enhancing behavior, or both! This includes: volunteering, offering kindness, anonymous donations, and anything else that is focused on lifting others up.

It can also look like offering a blessing. Blessings are universal and always aligned with a recipient's highest good. This means that, unlike prayer, you are not attaching to the outcome or imposing your will; you are simply offering the best to someone.

Remember, it takes courage to realize that it's not right to wish harm on others, even if you are experiencing pain yourself, perhaps especially then.

PART II:
Healing Karma

When it comes to Karma, the good news is that it can be healed, and, perhaps more importantly, you don't have to do it <u>with</u> the other person present. There are numerous ways to heal your Karma. To follow are three different approaches. But first, let's address why you should want to heal your Karma.

"When you truly understand karma, then you realize you are responsible for everything in your life."
— Keanu Reeves —

"Live a good and honorable life. Then, when you are older, you can look back and enjoy it a second time."
— Dalai Lama —

Healing anything in your life can lead to positive results. Most specifically, healing often leads to some measure of freedom. In the case of Karma, healing can bring forth forgiveness as well. Both forgiveness and healing create freedom.

Let's take a deeper look at Healing, Forgiveness, and Freedom and the roles they play in our lives:

🪷 <u>Healing is self-focused.</u> It's a process by which we connect more deliberately with ourself in meaningful ways, resulting in a greater sense of well-being.

🪷 <u>Forgiveness is other-focused.</u> It's a process that allows us to have a deeper understanding of our relationships as well as our behaviors and the behaviors of others. Engaging in forgiveness also results in greater connection to self, enhanced well-being, and freedom.

🪷 <u>Freedom is life/soul-focused.</u> Freedom is the result of deep connection to self and soul, which is often the result of the work done by healing past wounds, fixing dysfunctional patterns of behavior, and understanding the relationship one has to something greater—either the Divine, or on a more human level: Community or society. Freedom is the highest state of well-being one can achieve.

Healing is Self-Focused

*"The wound is the place
where the light enters you."*
— Rumi —

Asking for Help

Healing (including healing your Karma) is something you have to do yourself. However, you can enlist the help of others—especially professionals—to guide and support you on your healing journey. This is to say that nobody can do the work <u>for</u> you, but they can do it <u>with</u> you and alongside you.

Furthermore, asking for professional help is a sign of strength, not weakness. Reaching out to an expert when you are in need of help takes courage. All too often, people worry about the opinion of others, rather than worrying about their own healing journey. Sadly, there is still stigma around seeking help for mental health issues, though we do see evidence of that changing. Thankfully.

To find the best helping professional for you and your situation, it is best to consult with people you trust in your life. The important step is to start by asking. Additionally, there are many resources you can find to help you as you work to heal your Karma, which can include engaging in self-care practices.

"Healing is a daily event.
You can't 'go somewhere' to be healed;
you must go inward to be healed."
– Dr. Nicole LePera –

The Inward Journey

Healing Karma is self-focused because it requires an inward journey. Whether it's emotional, spiritual, or physical karmic healing that you seek, you will need to create a deeper connection to yourself; you will need to know yourself better and more clearly. This is especially true when you are focusing on healing spiritual or emotional Karma.

Though the inward journey can, at times, feel overwhelming, it's also true that the more you allow yourself to connect with and experience your feelings, thoughts, and emotions, the easier it will become. This is because the very nature of these things is that they are fluid, constantly in motion—just like Karma. By acknowledging your current thought, feeling, or emotion, you allow the next one in line to come forward, prompting the one you are experiencing to move on. This is part of the karmic healing journey: Recognizing that these types of human reactions are temporary and allowing them to be, instead of acting on them.

Forgiveness is Other-Focused

"To forgive is to set a prisoner free and discover that the prisoner was you."
— Lewis B. Smedes —

Unshackling Yourself

Forgiveness is most often about something external, which is why it's considered "other-focused." However, the effects of forgiveness are always internal. The external component is a requirement, because we are talking about Karma, which often involves others. There is, of course, self-forgiveness, but that is more often related to self-esteem or internal issues, which aren't often correlated to Karma, but rather are part of mental health.

As such, when discussing healing Karma, forgiveness is a tool that can be used to "unshackle" yourself from another, and take a step onto the path of karmic healing. To do this, one must realize three simple truths:

🪷 <u>Forgiveness is not one-and-done.</u> Though forgiveness requires a single initial step, it often also needs ongoing awareness on your part to shift your perspective.

🪷 <u>Forgiveness is always a choice.</u> Though it can feel hard to forgive someone, it is always an option. It is never removed from you, because it comes from within you.

🪷 <u>Forgiveness is not condoning or forgetting</u> an event. Instead it's about reclaiming your emotional power around the event, rather than letting it control you, while also helping you create boundaries, if necessary.

Choosing Forgiveness

When you make the choice to forgive, you are giving a gift to yourself and to your future! Forgiveness may require an external component to focus on (such as someone or something to forgive), but ultimately it is a solo act, and a choice you get to make.

Yes, forgiveness is a choice, and it's a choice that is always available to you, meaning: It's never too late, especially if you would like to heal your Karma.

Furthermore, it's never too soon. Since forgiveness is a gift you give yourself, the sooner you can do it, the better.

Finally, it bears noting that you can forgive without having to tell the other person. You can forgive them and move on, with or without sharing. So, if the idea of sharing forgiveness is holding you back, know that it doesn't need to. You can still forgive.

Freedom is Life and Soul-Focused

"Even death is not to be feared by one who has lived wisely."
— Buddha —

What is Freedom, Actually?

Freedom is about more than being free from oppression, fear, or any other low-frequency emotion or situation, though that is clearly important. Freedom is also about feeling empowered and having agency over your own life. The proverbial "pursuit of happiness" is most successful when it includes freedom.

When you work on healing your Karma and resolving your soul's lessons, you take steps towards that ultimate goal: Freedom. This is why Freedom is both Life- and Soul-Focused. It enhances your life in the present moment, just as it helps your soul in its evolution.

Healing your Karma is an important step to creating more freedom in your head and heart—more freedom in your life.

> "There is a wonderful mythical law of nature that the three things we crave most in life—happiness, freedom, and peace of mind—are always attained by giving them to someone else."
> — Peyton Conway March —

Investing in Yourself

If you think about your life in terms of mental and emotional real estate, you will find it easier to shift your perspective to one of "investing" rather than "coping with" or "managing" your life. This means that every time you take action and make the choice to heal your Karma, it is like making a deposit in your well-being account.

When life becomes about investing in yourself for your overall benefit, it gets easier to make choices that are aligned with healing your Karma. In addition to healing your Karma, the choices you make that result in more freedom can also serve to create good Karma for your future.

This is the ultimate goal and journey of the soul, to be free of Karma and return to oneness.

The Power of Invocations

"Everything that is in the heavens, on earth, and under the earth is penetrated with connectedness, penetrated with relatedness."
— Hildegard von Bingen —

What are Invocations?

There are many different types of invocations, all of which can be used for different purposes, including healing Karma. The intent behind each will matter as much as the words themselves, if not more. Though there are many, there are three that are commonly known that can be most effective. They are: Prayers, Mantras, and Blessings. Though all three can be considered a form of invocation, they differ in their context.

For example, blessings are more aligned with another person and provide you with an opportunity to express compassion and forgiveness. Similarly, a mantra is typically self-focused and provides you with guidance and reminders for you on your path in ways that are both thoughtful and consistent. Meanwhile, prayers can be both self- and other-focused.

How you use each of these interventions is up to you. Therefore, in order to choose what's best for your particular Karmic situation, it would be helpful to learn more about each of them and how they can help you heal your Karma and progress in your soul's journey.

Prayers

Though prayer is most often associated with religion, it doesn't have to be. Prayer is, in its simplest form, an expression of hope. Nothing more and nothing less. This simplicity does not in any way diminish the power of prayer or its significance, for hope is a very powerful force and energy. As such, prayer can be incredibly powerful, as well.

In general, there are three types of prayer: Connection, Gratitude, and Intercession. Though different, all three invoke something outside ourselves in their focus, such as a deity. For ease, we will refer to "God" as that deity.

A prayer of Connection is like sending a text or a love letter to God. It asks for nothing more than to be connected. A prayer of Gratitude is similar, but it adds a layer to the message. It includes an expression of appreciation for something. Both are more simple in their intent than the prayer of Intercession.

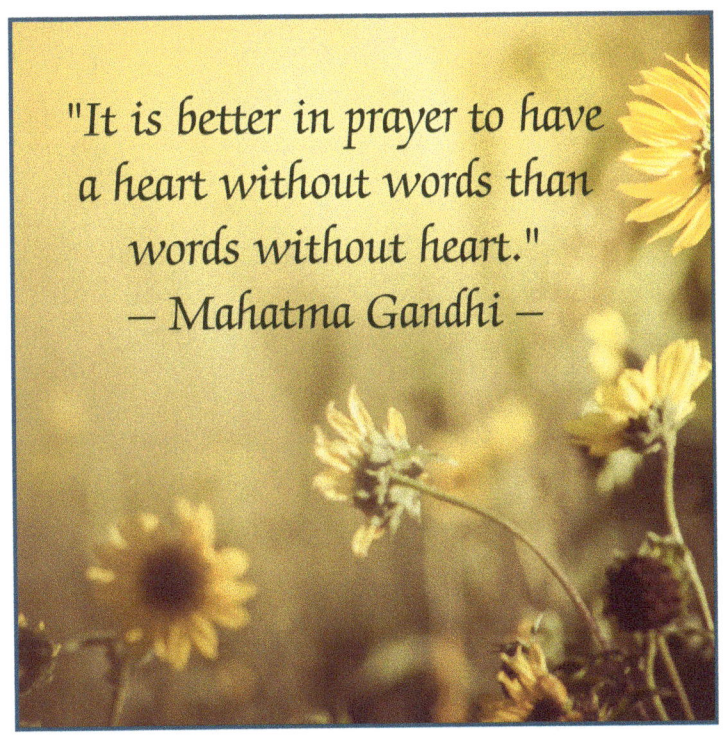

"It is better in prayer to have a heart without words than words without heart."
– Mahatma Gandhi –

A prayer of intercession is more like a plea for help. It's a request to intervene, usually on behalf of someone else.

It also carries a specific focus. These are the prayers that one hears when there is tragedy, loss, trauma, or fear. These prayers can also carry some sense of urgency to them. As such, they are less about connection and more about desperation and need.

When it comes to healing Karma, it is best to initially focus on prayers of Connection and Gratitude.

Mantras

A mantra is a message you are sending to your body and soul. Often received subliminally, it can serve as a reminder to your mind to align with something you have identified as important. As such, mantras are used as alignment tools. When it comes to healing Karma, mantras can be incredibly powerful interventions.

There is a simple truth in the universe that what you focus on will eventually appear. Time is the active variable. A mantra serves to help you focus. When you focus your energy, as well as your actions and behaviors, you can create significant change in your life. This is how you heal your Karma.

By committing to changing for the better, you are deliberately healing the Karma that you have collected in your life, or lifetimes.

"A mantra is a powerful tool to quiet the mind and focus your intention."
– Unknown –

Some examples of what this can look like include: being kinder to others (including yourself), doing service work, approaching your day with peace in your heart, managing your anger and reactivity, and so much more!

Mantras can help you do all of this by providing a tangible reminder of the commitments you have made to yourself and your future. You heal your Karma when you raise your awareness to the changes you wish to make and embody those choices.

Blessings

When you offer someone a blessing, you are living in a space of high compassion. This alignment with your higher self can only lead to more calm, inner peace, and well-being. This is a powerful way to heal your Karma.

Of course, it goes without saying that the intention behind the blessing matters. You cannot offer a blessing without meaning it and expect for it to do good. The blessing must be genuine and authentic, and when it is, incredible things can happen.

People often confuse blessings with prayers, though they carry a significant difference. The main difference between a blessing and a prayer is that a prayer maintains some measure of attachment to the outcome, whereas a blessing does not.

"You never know where a blessing can come from."
— Teena Marie —

When you offer someone a blessing, it is like making an anonymous donation. Though you may want to know about the outcome, you are not attached to it. The blessing, therefore, is one of the most altruistic actions you can take in healing your Karma and positively impacting your future.

Blessings are the gift you give away. Thankfully, they are infinite. There is no limit to how many blessings you can offer. What matters is that you are authentic in your offering.

Examples of Prayers to Heal Karma

For the purposes of simplicity, "God" will be used whenever referring to a deity.
<u>Please use whatever word or name you prefer.</u>

"Dear God, Please use me as a vessel of hope and healing for myself and others in this lifetime. Allow me to be an example for others in how to live a life in alignment with the highest good, for all. Thank you."

"Dear God, Thank you for allowing me to be of service to my world and community in ways that are benevolent to all who are in need. Give me eyes to see suffering and tools to help remedy it. Grant me patience and strength to be present and to choose a path that is for the greatest good. Amen."

> *"Karma is not just about the troubles, but also about surmounting them."*
> *– Rick Springfield –*

"Dear God, Thank you for the many blessings in my life, and for the continued blessings I receive. Thank you for helping me be a blessing to others just as I have received blessings. Amen."

"Dear God, I pray for the guidance and insight to focus my energy where it is most needed and to be a beacon of hope and a source of inspiration and help for others. Thank you for this life. Amen."

Examples of Mantras to Heal Karma

"I am a being of Light, and of the Light I choose to bring forth peace, harmony, and hope."

"I choose to participate in my life from a place of hope, joy, love, and alignment with all good things. Today and everyday."

"My life is a blessing to myself and others. I am aligned with joy, purpose, hope, and possibility."

"I am resilient, smart, and kind. I choose to align with that which I am at my core and know peace."

Examples of Blessings to Heal Karma

"May you find peace in your heart and healing in your journey."

"May you heal from within and know the peace that comes from unconditional love, joy, and hope."

"May we all choose a path aligned with community, hope, healing, and the peace that comes from living in harmony with respect and understanding. May we know love."

"May all beings be granted the Light of love and hope. May all heal and know joy."

Meditation and Healing

Meditation as a Pathway to Healing Karma

Meditation has been around for thousands of years, with the earliest evidence of written records presumed to be the ancient Indian Vedas (c. 1500 BCE). This implies that humans have had a need to go quietly inward for as long as we can remember, and definitely throughout all of the modern era.

There are many different forms of meditation, from the more formal practices, to the simple act of being present while sipping a cup of tea. Meditation, as a practice, is about presence more than anything else. This is why it is helpful in healing Karma. By being present, you are neither focusing on the past nor are you fixating on the future; you are in the here and now. By being present, you can best assess where you would like to make changes for the better. Awareness is the first step toward changing and healing your Karma. Being present is a requirement of awareness.

Engaging in a daily practice brings your mind and body into harmony and helps you have a clearer perspective. This will allow you to make more aligned decisions toward healing Karma.

"Meditation is the dissolution of thoughts in eternal awareness or pure consciousness without objectification, knowing without thinking, merging finitude in infinity."
– Voltaire –

Types of Meditation

Meditation can be both taught and learned. As such, it is important to find what works best for you and your situation. There are many types of meditation, but the two most common are:

- A daily (learned) practice of quieting the mind, such as Transcendental Meditation, breath work, or others
- Guided meditations from trusted sources, either in-person, or recorded

Daily Practice

To find the best daily practice for you, consider:

- Your environment
- Your time allowance
- Your commitment

It takes time to create a consistent practice, as well as a bit of trial and error. Be patient and the right model will show up.

Guided Meditation

To find the best guided meditation for you, consider:

- Trusted resources
- Purpose of the meditation
- Your personal limitations

Building a good repertoire of guided meditations should take your personal situation and preferences into account.

A Guided Meditation for Healing Karma

It would be best if you record this meditation (such as on your phone) and then listen to it after making yourself comfortable for this practice. (TIP: Speak slowly.)

Let's start with making sure you are comfortable. Whether you are sitting or lying down, see if you can feel your body connect with the surface beneath you. Feel the floor or the cushions against your skin. Feel yourself settle into this space, and as you settle, start with your breath. Take three slow, clearing breaths. With each breath, I invite you to feel your body soften into the surface beneath you. As you inhale, your muscles lift slightly, and then exhale, and feel yourself drop further into a comfortable and relaxed space. Breathe in... and breathe out. One more time: Breathe in... breathe out. Now, take a moment to just be in this space, allowing your body to breathe for itself.

As you feel yourself connected to the place where you are, envision yourself moving into a place that is beautiful, whatever that means for you. It's a gentle place, filled with softness and light. As you move into it, you hear something in the distance, like the sound of gently falling water. Using your breath, allow yourself to move toward the sound until you see a lovely small fountain in front of you. This is the fountain of clearing. Its waters hold healing properties, and it invites you to come closer.

Around the fountain, everything is shimmering, like gold and light at the same time. You are drawn to the peace you feel as you look at it, and you use your breath to move closer to the fountain's edge. As you stand directly in front of it, you can see your reflection in the water. It's a reflection of you at your happiest, calmest, and most joy-filled and peaceful. You smile as you see yourself in the waters.

Now, as you lean forward, reach your right hand into the water and place your left hand on your heart. Watch as you allow the golden light from the water move up into your hand and across your chest to your heart. Let the healing waters infuse your body with golden light as you hold your heart, continually breathing in peace, healing, and joy.

A Guided Meditation for Healing Karma

(continued)

Allow your body to release any fragments of completed Karma that it has been holding onto through the soles of your feet. Mother Earth will willingly take it and use it as raw energy to create something beautiful, something new. Releasing to the earth is a gift. Allow the golden light water to move throughout your body. If you feel it get stuck anywhere, use your breath to continue to move it on. Your breath can be a vessel for the healing waters.

When you feel that your whole body is filled with the golden light, lift your eyes to the space above you and see that all is good. Turn back to the fountain of water with gratitude, and thank the waters for bringing you on this journey of healing. Bow your head in appreciation as you pull your right hand out of the waters and let your left hand slowly fall away from your chest.

With your hands relaxed by your side, breathe deeply and feel your body and divine soul radiating with golden light. Breathe again and thank yourself for taking this step toward healing and love. And with your third breath, allow yourself to begin to come back to the present moment. The fountain will slowly move away from you now, and you will begin to feel the edges of your body again. You can feel the connection to the surface beneath you as you use your breath to wake your cells to the here and now.

You may wish to wiggle your toes and your fingers, your nose and your mouth. Move your shoulders up and down, as you breathe in again. Back in the space that you are in, allow your eyes to regain their sight as you take in your surroundings. Move your limbs and your torso to come fully back into your body, and take a deep clearing breath bringing yourself back to full consciousness. Pause for a moment, bringing your hands together in front of your heart, to say thank you to yourself for choosing to heal, then thanking the earth and the waters for helping you clear and heal your Karma.

With gratitude.

Scan here to purchase an expanded recorded version,

Life by Design or Default

"Karma, when properly understood, is just the mechanics through which consciousness manifests."
— Deepak Chopra —

The Power of Choice

At the end of the day, Karma may be a universal law, but it can also be a compass through which you guide and create your life. It is, in that sense, like a roadmap to a journey you have not yet taken, but one that has all the best landmarks (and detours) already listed. In other words, it's the tool by which you can create your best life imaginable—both in this lifetime and the next.

How do you create this guide? It all boils down to choice. You can either live your life deliberately or by default.

Living by Default

The person who lives life by default is the one who often finds themself being more reactionary than not. They perhaps always feel like a victim, or like life is happening <u>to</u> them. Living by default is what happens when we allow our environment (people, situations, etc.) to make our decisions for us.

This can build resentment, anger, and frustration—which can lead to us wanting to wish harm on someone, because we can't see a way out of the pain. When we feel backed into a corner, we sometimes feel the need to fight our way out by harming those we either blame for our position, or who we feel are in our way, without realizing that it's not usually a corner. Either way, wishing harm is never a good option, because of Karma. There is a better way: Living deliberately.

> *"If your actions were to boomerang back on you instantly, would you still act the same?"*
> — *Alexandra Katehakis* —

Living Deliberately

Living deliberately is about raising your awareness to your life in such a way that you begin to feel the most empowered. In other words, you get to choose—<u>and are choosing</u>—how you show up, who you are in relationship with, and how you are interacting with people and situations in your life.

This is not selfish; this is about knowing yourself and having good boundaries. It's also about not taking on someone else's Karma. Though it may feel difficult at first because you're not used to it, the more you practice living deliberately, the easier it becomes.

If, for example, you already feel backed into a corner, it will take some patience and a dedication to being consistent in your choices to create a different way. Mantras can help with this. They serve as the daily reminders of what you actually want—what you are actually choosing—which is a life with freedom at its core.

Healing Karma (and creating good Karma) is easier when you choose to live your life deliberately. The best news is that it's a choice you can make every day.

"The meaning of karma is in the intention. The intention behind action is what matters."
— The Bhagavad Gita —

In Conclusion

Understanding Karma is about understanding yourself—what drives you, what you are feeling, who you are, what you want and why. When you take the time to connect with your inner being in a direct and compassionate way, you empower yourself to make different choices. These choices can lead to healing, forgiveness, and freedom, which all leads to better Karma for both the present and the future.

Focusing on your Karma is one of the best gifts you can give yourself and the world. As you heal, you also remove opportunities and the desire to hurt or harm others; harming others is never a good idea and rarely results in positive results. Choosing to heal yourself, instead of harming others, further reduces your karmic footprint.

This approach creates more harmony in your life, which can only be of benefit. Ultimately, though healing Karma starts with you, it can have positive ripple effects throughout the world. Thankfully.

May you find the courage, peace, and joy you seek as you journey toward understanding—and healing—your Karma.

> *"The quality of your life is based
> on the choices you make."*
> — Martina E. Faulkner —

About the Author

Martina E. Faulkner is a cross-genre author whose work focuses primarily on exploring what it means to be human, both the unique and the universal. She holds a trifecta in the mental health/healing world as a therapist, certified life coach, and Reiki Master Teacher. This distinctive background allows her to draw on her professional and personal experience in her writing, whether fiction, nonfiction, or poetry.

A self-proclaimed Anglophile, Martina drinks tea daily, loves walks in nature, and enjoys looking at beautiful images from the British Isles while dreaming up her next book. You can read her regular column "Unique and Universal" on Substack, follow her on Instagram and Facebook @martinaefaulkner, or visit martinaefaulkner.com.

As a children's author Martina's debut children's book, <u>When the World Went Quiet</u>, was given as a gift to Sir David Attenborough, who referred to it as "charming."

Other Books by Martina

Love and Pain: *Poetry From the Chambers of My Heart*

What if..?: *How to Create the Life You Want Using the Power of Possibility*

50 and F*ck It!: *Learn How You Can Let Go, Stand In Your Boots, and Truly Live!*

Infinite In My Heart: *Poems of Love, Loss, and Hope*

Me: 365: *A 5-Year Question-A-Day Journal*

The Author's Journey: *Your Roadmap to Navigating and Understanding the Publishing Industry*

Crafting the Perfect College Essay: *Write Your Best Essay in 3 Easy Steps*

Children's Books by Martina E. Faulkner as Tia Martina

When the World Went Quiet
Princess Wigglebottom and the Forgotten Christmas